Manager

CAREERS WITH CHARACTER

Careers with Character

Manager

by Ann E. Vitale

Glen Burnie H. S. Media Center

MASON CREST PUBLISHERS

Mason Crest Publishers Inc.
370 Reed Road
Broomall, Pennsylvania 19008
(866) MCP-BOOK (toll free)
www.masoncrest.com

First printing
1 2 3 4 5 6 7 8 9 10
Library of Congress Cataloging-in-Publication Data on file at the Library of Congress.
ISBN 1-59084-317-7
        1-59084-327-4 (series)

Design by Lori Holland.
Composition by Bytheway Publishing Services, Binghamton, New York.
Printed and bound in the Hashemite Kingdom of Jordan.

Photo Credits:
Comstock: pp. 51, 59, 63, 69, 70, 72, 79
Corbis: pp. 4, 6, 7, 14, 16, 23, 56
Corel: pp. 20, 22, 30, 48, 58
Digital Stock: pp. 9, 49, 68, cover
PhotoDisc: pp. 8, 12, 15, 18, 24, 25, 31, 35, 38, 40, 41, 42, 43, 46, 53, 60, 61, 66, 76,
    78, 80, 81, 83
Viola Ruelke Gommer: pp. 28, 32

CONTENTS

We each leave a fingerprint on the world.
Our careers are the work we do in life.
Our characters are shaped by the choices
we make to do good.
When we combine careers with character,
we touch the world with power.

INTRODUCTION

by Dr. Cheryl Gholar
and Dr. Ernestine G. Riggs

In today's world, the awesome task of choosing or staying in a career has become more involved than one would ever have imagined in past decades. Whether the job market is robust or the demand for workers is sluggish, the need for top-performing employees with good character remains a priority on most employers' lists of "must have" or "must keep." When critical decisions are being made regarding a company or organization's growth or future, job performance and work ethic are often the determining factors as to who will remain employed and who will not.

How does one achieve success in one's career and in life? Victor Frankl, the Austrian psychologist, summarized the concept of success in the preface to his book *Man's Search for Meaning* as: "The unintended side-effect of one's personal dedication to a course greater than oneself." Achieving value by responding to life and careers from higher levels of knowing and being is a specific goal of teaching and learning in "Careers with Character." What constitutes success for us as individuals can be found deep within our belief system. Seeking, preparing, and attaining an excellent career that aligns with our personality is an outstanding goal. However, an excellent career augmented by exemplary character is a visible expression of the human need to bring meaning, purpose, and value to our work.

Career education informs us of employment opportunities, occupational outlooks, earnings, and preparation needed to perform certain tasks. Character education provides insight into how a person of good character might choose to respond, initiate an action, or perform specific tasks in the presence of an ethical dilemma. "Careers with Character" combines the two and teaches students that careers are more than just jobs. Career development is incomplete without character development. What better way to explore careers and character than to make them a single package to be opened, examined, and reflected upon as a means of understanding the greater whole of who we are and what work can mean when one chooses to become an employee of character?

Character can be defined simply as "who you are even when no one else is around." Your character is revealed by your choices and actions. These bear your personal signature, validating the story of who you are. They are the fingerprints you leave behind on the people you meet and know; they are the ideas you bring into reality. Your choices tell the world what you truly believe.

Character, when viewed as a standard of excellence, reminds us to ask ourselves when choosing a career: "Why this particular career, for what purpose, and to what end?" The authors of "Careers with Character" knowledgeably and passionately, through their various vignettes, enable one to experience an inner journey that is both intellectual and moral. Students will find themselves, when confronting decisions in real life, more prepared, having had experiential learning opportunities through this series. The books, however, do not separate or negate the individual good from the academic skills or intellect needed to perform the required tasks that lead to productive career development and personal fulfillment.

Each book is replete with exemplary role models, practical strategies, instructional tools, and applications. In each volume, individuals of character work toward ethical leadership, learning how to respond appropriately to issues of not only right versus wrong, but issues of right versus right, understanding the possible benefits and consequences of their decisions. A wealth of examples is provided.

What is it about a career that moves our hearts and minds toward fulfilling a dream? It is our character. The truest approach to finding out who we are and what illuminates our lives is to look within. At the very

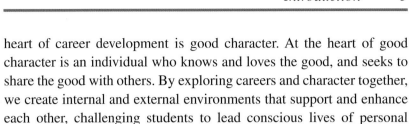

heart of career development is good character. At the heart of good character is an individual who knows and loves the good, and seeks to share the good with others. By exploring careers and character together, we create internal and external environments that support and enhance each other, challenging students to lead conscious lives of personal quality and true richness every day.

Is there a difference between doing the right thing, and doing things right? Career questions ask, "What do you know about a specific career?" Character questions ask, "Now that you know about a specific career, what will you choose to do with what you know?" "How will you perform certain tasks and services for others, even when no one else is around?" "Will all individuals be given your best regardless of their socioeconomic background, physical condition, ethnicity, or religious beliefs?" Character questions often challenge the authenticity of what we say we believe and value in the workplace and in our personal lives.

Character and career questions together challenge us to pay attention to our lives and not fall asleep on the job. Career knowledge, self-knowledge, and ethical wisdom help us answer deeper questions about the meaning of work; they give us permission to transform our lives. Personal integrity is the price of admission.

The insight of one "ordinary" individual can make a difference in the world—if that one individual believes that character is an amazing gift to uncap knowledge and talents to empower the human community. Our world needs everyday heroes in the workplace—and "Careers with Character" challenges students to become those heroes.

Dave Thomas was a successful manager who built his career on the principles of a good character.

1

JOB REQUIREMENTS

*A successful career in management is built
on many things . . . including character.*

In 1932 a baby boy was born to a young woman. She wasn't married and did not have enough education to get more than the lowest paying jobs—so she gave up her newborn son for adoption in order that he might have a better life than she could provide. Mr. and Mrs. Thomas, the baby's adoptive parents, called him David. Dave Thomas grew up to be the founder of Wendy's restaurant chain.

Unfortunately, Dave's adoptive mother died when he was only five years old. North America was still feeling the aftereffects of the **Great Depression**, and David's father had to move frequently in search of work, taking young Dave with him to small apartments and trailer parks. When Dave Thomas was 12, he got his first restaurant job to help the family make ends meet. The owners of the business were immigrants and taught Dave some valuable lessons about striving for success. They were honest, compassionate, hardworking people, who taught the young boy some good character values.

Dave quit school when he was 15 and worked full time in another restaurant. He was very responsible for his age and took every opportunity to learn about the business. In his autobiography, Dave admits that, despite his ultimate success, dropping out of school was a big mistake. His unique inborn intelligence, creativity, and drive made him a suc-

Management is defined as getting things done through other people. Managers' success is measured by their ability to get other people to perform at their best. Managers who lead by good example, who exhibit the character traits of fairness, compassion, trustworthiness, integrity, and justice, can inspire others to make ethical decisions that benefit the group—and what benefits the group will benefit the individual.

cessful and wealthy business manager at a fairly young age, but some people looked down on him for his lack of education. He wondered what more he could have accomplished if he had stayed in school. He also worried that other young people might drop out, thinking they could succeed the same as he had; he knew his story was the exception to the rule, much as it is the rare high school football player who makes it to the Super Bowl.

Dave Thomas spoke at many high school and college graduations, urging young people to get

Dave Thomas, like all good managers, was successful because he helped others perform at their best.

Dave Thomas didn't just make hamburgers—he used his business success to bring public attention to many worthy causes.

all the education they could, not only to be productive citizens but to be better, well-rounded persons. He took to heart Benjamin Franklin's advice, "Well done is better than well said," and studied to pass the exam to obtain his high school equivalency certificate, although 43 years late. "We have over 4,000 restaurants today," he said in an interview, "but it might have been 8,000 had I stayed in school."

He used his fame and recognition as Wendy's most powerful manager to bring public attention to adoption and the need for all children to have a stable, loving home. He taught the values and ***ethics*** of business management to all his employees, and he respected the opinions of the newest and youngest workers if they had an idea about a better way to do things. He extended the dignity of work to the disadvantaged and handicapped.

Dave Thomas died in January 2002, at the age of 69. During his life he testified in front of Congress in favor of a tax credit for families adopting children. He lent his name and fame to causes ranging from cancer research to encouraging high school graduates to work, save,

Some managers may not have any particular educational background; instead, they are successful because of a variety of skills and past experiences.

and find funding on their own to go to college. He believed in helping those who made the maximum effort to help themselves. He was an excellent natural manager.

Like Dave Thomas, many who become business owners or department managers never trained specifically for that job. On-the-job training is common. However, to do a really good job, some educational paths make the goal easier to reach.

Certain management careers require a very specific educational program. School districts usually mandate that principals have a Master of Education degree. To be a superintendent of a school district, a Ph.D. is often necessary. Supervisors of hospitals and nursing homes, as well as related health fields, have educational and licensing requirements set by government regulators.

If a career as a manager in a large corporation is a goal, a college degree with courses in financial management, marketing, business law, business policy and ethics, operations and production management, statistics, and economics is recommended. If the company is a manufacturer, a degree in chemical, mechanical, ceramic, or industrial engineering with a Master of Business Administration degree (MBA) might be the way to go. Frequently an engineer, chemist, or computer science major begins employment with a company, and if he or she shows an interest in or aptitude for management, the company will help pay for the advanced business degree or additional courses necessary for promotion. Most of these courses are available at night or on weekends. There are even colleges offering courses on the Internet.

The ability to communicate

Competencies and character traits needed for success:

- Retail store manager: self-control, conscientiousness, empathy, service orientation
- Bank manager: confidentiality, respect for all clients regardless of economic circumstances
- IRS middle manager: communication skills, teamwork, attention to details, diligence
- Law enforcement official: self-control, compassion, fairness, integrity
- Food company distribution manager: leadership, analytical skills, communication skills

A good manager is able to work well with others.

There is no such thing as business ethics. There is only ethics.

Your character is defined by what you do, not what you say you believe.
Every choice you make helps define the kind of person you are choosing to be.
Good character requires doing the right thing, even when it is costly or risky.
You don't have to take the worst behavior of others as a standard for yourself.
You can choose to be better than that.

Organizations wishing to hire managers look for these traits:

• Effective listening, writing, and speaking
• Willingness to learn new procedures
• Pride in work
• Cooperation with a team
• Empathy

ideas orally and in writing, in good standard English, is especially important. Much of today's business is done in the *global economy*, and poor grammar, vocabulary, and spelling are frowned upon by the well-educated managers of foreign companies.

Advancement skills can also be learned in a non-degree program, and seminars are readily available through various business organizations. The idea of how to be a good manager is changing from the old style of simply giving orders to subordinates (top-down management), to the new team approach that considers input from all employees concerned with the decisions (bottom-up management). The business world is fast realizing that character counts—and the brilliant MBA holder may be passed over for a promotion in favor of the person who demonstrates these traits:

• integrity and trustworthiness
• respect and compassion
• justice and fairness
• responsibility
• courage
• self-discipline and diligence
• citizenship

Like Dave Thomas, not all managers have a degree in business or a related field. Many worked their way up from the bottom, and their expertise was gained by experience rather than from any college degree. But most truly successful managers share one thing in common—a character that's built on the core qualities listed above.

I am the maker of my own fortune.

—Tecumseh, Shawnee chief

A manager of a busy clothing store will also have other opportunities to touch the world with integrity.

2

INTEGRITY AND TRUSTWORTHINESS

Keep true; never be ashamed of doing right;
decide on what you think is right
and stick to it.

Jean Cooke was a busy woman. She owned her own clothing store and still found time to serve on the board of directors of the animal shelter and on the board of the county cancer society. People like Jean who are in management positions frequently find themselves in demand for positions on charitable boards. Some are sought because their names give the organizations prestige. Others seek the posts because it looks good on their personal resumes. Many are serious about the contribution their business **acumen** gives to the board. Their experience helps balance the more emotional and less practical volunteers. Management skills are valuable in steering meeting agendas toward accomplishments and recognizing the talents of other members.

However, management experience does not always translate readily from private business to boards of charities. In Jean's clothing store, her three employees understood the way things were to be done and usually obeyed Jean's directions. But the charities' boards were made up of volunteers, some of whom had no business sense and were guided by high ideals and personal feelings, with little understanding that deci-

Being able to work well on a committee is part of many managers' jobs.

sions, especially on limited budgets, had to be made based on needs and facts.

This year it was Jean's turn to serve in a position on the County Charitable Trust Committee. Every spring this trust accepted applications from any county charity that needed funds. And who has ever heard of a charity that didn't need funds?

According to Rushworth M. Kidder, author of *How Good People Make Tough Choices,* people often use three principles to resolve *ethical dilemmas.* These principles are:

1. Ends-based thinking: What is best for the greatest number of people?
2. Rule-based thinking: What is your highest sense of what is right?
3. Care-based thinking: Will you do what others want you to do?

The money the trust committee distributed came from donations given by individuals and businesses through the United Way and from corporate grants. The funds were allocated according to a formula based on how much money the charity spent the previous year and how many people in the county it served. Representatives of the charities were allowed to be present at the trust committee meeting to further explain why they were entitled to part of the money.

Character education helps people become:

Conscious of the right things to do.

Committed to doing the right thing.

Competent in doing the right thing.

Jean had objected at her cancer society board meeting when she found out that the figures the society reported for people it served were inflated. The secretary counted not only those people present at club meetings such as Professional Women and the Lions Club when cancer

Managers must be able to handle money wisely, determining the best way for each dollar to be spent.

People with integrity:

- Admit their own mistakes and confront unethical actions in others.
- Act ethically and are above reproach.
- Build trust through their reliability and authenticity.

Adapted from *Working with Emotional Intelligence* by D. Goleman.

prevention programs were presented, but also every patient who visited every dentist's office where oral cancer brochures were in the waiting rooms.

"I don't think that practice is true to our mission," Jean argued. "We don't know if the patients picked up a brochure, or understood it if they read it. I don't feel comfortable with counting them as being educated."

"But we need the funding. It will help pay for other services, like transporting patients to chemotherapy treatments, and renting wheelchairs and hospital beds for home use. You know requests are increasing." Barbara Fulton, who was president of the board, was very persua-

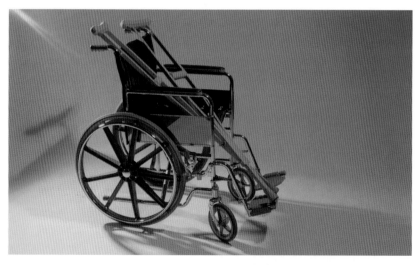

While serving on charity boards, managers may have the opportunity to help supply equipment and services to people with handicapping conditions.

> **Evaluate Options from Various Perspectives**
>
> - Which option will produce the most good and do the least harm?
> - Which option respects the rights and dignity of all **stakeholders**? Even if not everyone gets all they want, will everyone still be treated fairly?
> - Which option would promote the common good and help all participate fully in the goods we share as a society, as a community, as a company, or as a family?
> - Which option would enable the deepening or development of those virtues or character traits that we value as individuals and as a society?
>
> From the Markkula Center for Applied Ethics.

sive. Barbara was also a regular customer in Jean's clothing store and often brought her grown daughters with her to shop, too.

When Jean attended the board meeting for the animal shelter, she found their figures to apply for trust funds were gathered in an acceptable manner, reporting the money spent for the year and carefully counting the people who came to the shelter to adopt pets. School children and scout troops who toured the shelter with their teachers were also counted. The shelter was having trouble paying its bills and in danger of having to reduce the number of days it was open for people to bring animals in or to adopt them. The closest shelter was 40 miles away.

When the County Charitable Trust Committee met, the members had to consider many applications for funding. If the applying organization met the standards for a nonprofit charity and the paperwork was in order, the organization would be eligible for a percentage of the money according to the formula. One organization after the other was approved for its share of the funds. The Boy Scouts and Girl Scouts, Office for the Elderly, Red Cross, animal shelter, and others passed muster.

If you have integrity you will:

- Stand up for your beliefs.
- Follow your conscience.
- Be honorable and upright.
- Live by your principles no matter what others say
- Have the courage to do what is right and to try new things even when it is hard or costly.
- Build and guard your reputation.

The cancer society's application was read and put up for comment and a vote. The society would receive the largest percentage of the money based on expenditures and number of people served. Jean had only minutes to decide to vote for or against the application.

What should Jean do? If she exposes what she considers a technically fraudulent report, she will go against the will of the majority of the board of directors of the cancer society. This would certainly anger Barbara, who is also a customer in Jean's store. But Jean is also a member of the animal shelter board, and she knows how badly they could use a larger percentage of the money. If the cancer society gets a

Integrity is built on a careful examination of both the external situation and your internal sense of what is right.

larger share, it means all the other groups get a little less. What would you do?

Here is another way to look at this problem. If you had just $20 to give away, would you donate it to send an inner-city child to day camp, pay for food and shelter for an abused dog, or give it to a family whose mother had cancer? Would your choice be different if you discovered the family's financial needs were legitimate, but they had lied about some aspect of the mother's condition in order to influence your decision? Should your decision be affected by others' dishonesty—or should it be based solely on need (or some other quality)?

> Integrity is choosing to do the right thing. Trustworthiness is choosing to do the right thing again, and again, and again.

As the person who manages the distribution of charitable funds, is it acceptable to use statements that aren't exactly the truth, to gain an advantage for something you really believe in? What do you think?

We cannot have perfection. We have few saints. But we must have honest [people]. . . . We must have unselfish, far-seeing leadership or we fail.

—*W.E.B DuBois*

Fire or other disasters can present managers with hard decisions.

3

RESPECT AND COMPASSION

Ethics is not concerned with descriptions of the way things are, but prescriptions for the way they ought to be.

On December 11, 1995, Aaron Feuerstein was in a restaurant in Boston with his family and friends. The successful businessman was 70 years old that day, celebrating his close ties with his family and associates as they sang "Happy Birthday" to him. They were unaware that 25 miles away, an explosion had ripped through Feuerstein's textile factory and a fire was raging. Workers were hurt; six fire companies were fighting the blaze in zero-degree cold and high winds; fire hoses were freezing; and the fire was winning.

Thirty-three employees were injured, some seriously, and three factory buildings, 600,000 square feet of manufacturing floor space, were reduced to rubble. It appeared that everything was lost.

Many years before, Aaron Feuerstein's immigrant grandfather had founded Malden Mills, as the factory complex was called, in the nearby town of Malden. Its owner had stubbornly hung on as many fabric mills moved to the southern states or even to foreign countries where costs of power, water, and nonunion labor were cheaper, and now it was one of the few textile companies remaining in New England.

Malden Mills was an important manufacturer of the new fleece fabric. The mill made a lot of money supplying this popular fabric to

21

L.L. Bean and Patagonia as well as other sportswear companies. Now Mr. Feuerstein could take the $300 million the insurance company would pay for the fire damage and build a new factory somewhere else where it would be even more profitable.

Some employees had been with the company for more than 30 years. Whole families worked for Malden Mills. The workers, many of them immigrants from Portugal, Quebec, and various Hispanic countries, were sure this was the end of 3,400 jobs.

Smoke was still rising from the ruins, and injured men were still in the hospital, when Mr. Feuerstein called a meeting in the high school gym. Grown men as well as women were crying. They were sure they knew what their boss was going to say to them.

What they heard next did not stop their tears, but it changed them from tears of despair and fear to tears of hope and gratitude, and, yes, disbelief, as Aaron Feuerstein made promises.

He promised to pay every worker's wages for the rest of December

Managing a clothing factory requires respect and compassion for each individual worker.

A compassionate manager has opportunities to help workers' improve their financial situations.

or until unemployment paperwork was processed. He would give each employee $275 as a Christmas gift. And he would rebuild Malden Mills, right where it had stood before the fire; and give as many people as possible their old jobs back. If new equipment took some of those old jobs away, he would pay to retrain the people for different jobs.

If Aaron Feuerstein faced an ethical dilemma before he made those promises, it was an easy one for him to solve. Throughout his long life as a manager, he had already chosen the sort of character he wanted to have. Respect and compassion for his employees had

You do not have to agree with people in order to respect them. Talking and listening are two ways to practice respect. Appreciating their ideas and accomplishments is another.

Jackie Robinson, the first African American big league professional baseball player said: "I'm not concerned with your liking or disliking me. . . . All I ask is that you respect me as a human being."

The manager of the furniture department in a large store doesn't only sell furniture; he also must be able to interact with others—customers, coworkers, and supervisors—with compassion and respect.

become a habit. "Those workers are depending on me," he said in an interview for *Life* magazine. "The community is depending on me. My customers are depending on me. And my family." He continued to explain that treating the workers fairly is good for everyone. "The employees are not an expense. I sell the quality . . . that we make. The workers make that quality. When you do the right thing, you'll probably end up more profitable than if you did wrong. It speaks poorly for society that standards have decreased to the point that I'm considered superb."

Respect and compassion are two-way streets, however. Consider the following scenario where two department store managers were refused promotions because of poor reviews by their superiors.

Bob, the furniture department manager, reacted with shock, embarrassment, and anger. He did not like his boss, who had often criticized him in front of customers and coworkers. It seemed there was no way to please the man. Bob had fantasies about doing bad things to his boss, like scratching his new car or vandalizing his house. Bob went to work

The International Association of Lions Clubs Code of Ethics:

To seek success and to demand all fair **remuneration** or profit as my just due, but to accept no profit or success at the price of my own self-respect lost because of unfair advantage taken or because of questionable acts on my part.

To remember that in building up my business it is not necessary to tear down another's; to be loyal to my clients or customers and true to myself.

Whenever a doubt arises as to the right or ethics of my position or action towards others, to resolve such doubts against myself.

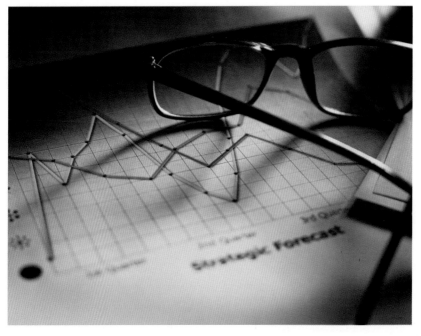

As a manager, it should be possible to build up the business without tearing down others.

the next day, walked with his head down, and didn't speak to anyone unless he had to answer a question. He mumbled insults about his boss where he knew the other employees would hear him. He thought about quitting his job, even though he was sure the bad review was not his fault.

Ken, the kitchen appliance manager, was also shocked when he wasn't promoted. He went home and talked to his wife. As he talked about his disappointment, he realized he had not been doing his best—and that meant he had not been treating his employer with respect. He and his boss had different ideas and argued a lot, but Ken respected him enough that he asked for an appointment with his superior. They made a list of the things each liked about the other and another list of their disagreements. These lists helped them each to feel compassion for the other's situation. In the end, they shook hands and agreed to a three-month trial of some new ideas each had contributed during the discussion.

Which man do you think understands the most about respect and compassion?

Pity is often mistaken for compassion.
Pity is heavy.
Compassion lifts.
If you want others to be happy, practice compassion.
If you want to be happy, practice compassion.

—*the Dalai Lama*

The manager of a nursing home must be able to treat both employees and residents with fairness and respect.

4

JUSTICE AND FAIRNESS

People who are fair and just will challenge
bias and intolerance.

Marie Grant arrived at work early Monday morning, her first day as manager of the Lakeview Senior Living Center. She wanted to give herself time to review Lakeview's thick handbook of policies and procedures. Marie had not expected a management position that came with such strict detailed instructions in addition to the government regulations.

I guess they need this, she thought, flipping through the book. *The owners have been in this business longer than I have, that's for sure.* Lakeview was known for a high turnover of staff and managers, and a handbook was supposed to assure that the residents were always treated the same and the workers knew what was expected of them.

Keeping the staff, residents, and their families content was quite a balancing act, at least according to the manager who had just resigned. The previous manager had told Marie the policy book was the way to keep order. Even so, he reported, the staff members grumbled about schedules and complained about favoritism.

Marie's last job had been in a residential home for adults with mental handicaps, and she had a system she called "management by walking around." If she spent enough time in every nook and cranny of the home, her presence was so commonplace that the staff behaved as they

29

A fair manager listens to workers' concerns.

normally would if not being observed by "the boss." This management style offered opportunities for informal reviews and information gathering. The caregivers soon found she was willing to listen to their suggestions as well as complaints. Now Marie had a new staff with whom to get acquainted, and from what she had heard, they could be a cantankerous crew.

Marie ate lunch in the dining hall that day and watched the residents and the staff. All the aides seemed genuinely interested in the well-being of the seniors in their care. While she ate, Marie noticed Angelique and Delia, the two aides who were in the United States on work visas from Jamaica. The two women met in the center hall and talked quietly, but their tight lips and sideways glance at another aide passing by made it quite plain that all was not well with the caregiving staff.

On Tuesday, Marie visited the kitchen and passed some time casually with the cooks and clean-up crew. They were a jolly bunch; almost like a family. They were all very kind to Gina, a ***Down syndrome*** teenager who performed well the tasks she was assigned.

Marie was pleased to see that Lakeview's owners were fair enough that they were willing to employ someone with mental handicaps, and she was impressed by the kitchen staff's acceptance of Gina. Marie knew that fairness and justice were an important part of any successful work environment.

On the way back to her office, Marie again saw Angelique and Delia whispering together. *Maybe they have a family problem or something,* Marie thought and was ready to dismiss the incident from her mind until she heard Delia say, "She thinks she is so smart. I'll fix her. I'll call in sick. You, too. Then what'll she do?"

Oh, no, thought Marie, *not trouble already.*

When she got back to her office, she asked Betty, her secretary, if there was anything she needed to know about conflicts within the day shift staff.

Betty didn't hesitate. "It's the schedule. Almost always the schedule. We do everything according to the policy book, but there's still trouble. We make up the schedule and post it a month ahead. Weekends

Scheduling is a big responsibility—one that should be accomplished fairly for everyone concerned.

> As managers, managing is what we do on a daily basis
> that communicates the behavior we expect.
> Counseling pinpoints opportunities for improved behavior.
> Behavior is what people actually do.
> Consequences are the result of what we choose to do.

and holidays are covered in regular rotation, according to the policy book, just like any other day of the week. But Sue and Vera and Debbie have some deal worked out where they cover for each other or talk Angelique or Delia into switching, but then they never seem to be able to reciprocate—and Angelique and Delia are fed up. The rest of the aides complain, too. I suspect that Sue and Vera and Debbie are taking advantage of Angelique and Delia, because the Jamaican women don't understand the system as well, and they don't speak English perfectly. But it doesn't help to get involved. By the time you've figured out

Workers may need a chance to air their complaints, confident that their manager will listen and be fair.

Justice is often portrayed as a woman with a scale who weighs life's dilemmas fairly.

A person who practices justice. . .

- recognizes the honor and respect due to all occupations that are useful to society.
- is fair to employer, employees, associates, competitors, customers, the public, and all those with whom he or she has a business or professional relationship.
- offers *vocational* talents to provide opportunities for young people, to work for the relief of the special needs of others, and to improve the quality of life in his or her community.

Adapted from the Rotary International Declaration.

who's causing the trouble, they're usually gone. We have a ***turnover*** problem."

"Why do you think that is?" Marie asked.

Betty worded her answer carefully. "The pay for one thing. You have to be pretty dedicated to do what these women do for what they're paid. And the lack of benefits is discouraging, but it's why most of the staff is held to 30 hours a week. That's part time, really. And some get ***burned out***. I can't say as I blame them, especially if they care for a few of the very time-consuming or cranky residents. It's a wonder the five Jamaican women are still working here, but I guess maybe they don't have much choice. They get pushed around—given the most difficult residents to care for."

Wednesday morning Marie walked past the door of the employee lounge as the aides were getting ready for the day's work. An argument was going on, and almost everyone, it seemed, had something to say.

Angelique's voice was easily recognized. "I have to work Thanksgiving and Christmas. Both. That's not fair."

Debbie wasn't very sympathetic. "That's the way the schedule worked out."

Angelique was not happy. "Debbie, you owe me for two Sundays I changed for you. Why can't you take one of the holidays?"

Marie had heard enough. She went back to her office, and by the time Betty came in, Marie had a plan.

"Put a note on the door of the lounge saying that all aides should be there 15 minutes before the shift ends. And I'll need the names and phone numbers of day shift aides that aren't here today. We are going to democratic scheduling."

"But the policy book tells us how to make up the schedules." Betty protested.

Marie opened the bottom drawer of her desk, picked up the policy book, and dropped it into the drawer. Then she took out an empty sheet of paper. "Apparently, the policy doesn't work very well here. It isn't fair and it encourages the workers to be selfish. I think if we start with a blank paper for the schedule, instead of the policy book, the workers will listen to each other—and hopefully they will hear the injustice of

A good manager helps people to work together so that the organization can be profitable for everyone concerned.

putting people into categories. We will create the schedule as we go along, based on the workers' needs rather than a list of rules. After all, these people have chosen to be caregivers. I prefer to believe they will also care about each other."

Do you think Marie's plan to let the aides work out their own schedule will work? Will it solve all the problems? Marie wants to create a work atmosphere where people are treated with justice and fairness, regardless of their nationality. What else can Marie do so the employees at Lakeview are treated more fairly?

It is surely our duty to do all the good we can to all the people we can in all the ways we can.

—William Barclay

Managers come in many shapes and sizes; they are found everywhere from enormous corporations that make millions of dollars—to fast-food restaurants where the profit margin may be only a few cents.

5

RESPONSIBILITY

*Not everyone will understand if you choose
to act responsibly—but the consequences
of responsible actions are worth the cost.*

Matt was a senior in high school and had just a few more courses necessary for college entrance. He was excited about the catalogs arriving in the mail and had downloaded the applications from the web sites of the schools he hoped would consider him for next fall's freshman class. It was only September, but he knew it would be a lot of work to fill out the forms, get references, write his essay, and find sources of financial assistance.

He did have control over one place for financial help, and that was his job at the Burger Castle. His parents agreed that this year, if his grades stayed at Bs or above, he could work more hours, including nights as well as weekends. Mr. Bonito liked Matt and was in favor of letting him work as many hours as the young man thought he could handle.

September had been busy at the BC, as the kids called the Burger Castle. After school, carloads of teens lined up at the drive-in window, and families occupied the few tables inside. Matt and the three others had to scramble to keep up with the rush. After 6:00, it slowed down a little, and by 10:00 there were few customers unless there was a sports event or a good movie, then another small crowd came to the drive-in window for late snacks. The BC closed at 10:30, and the workers tried to have the cleaning done soon after. Usually the last to leave were Mr. Bonito and the one other employee on the late crew. Matt was a night owl and didn't mind that most weekend nights he was the late worker.

In early October, Mr. Bonito was more talkative than usual as he and Matt checked off the closing list. The rest rooms were disinfected and resupplied, the temperatures of the refrigerators and freezer recorded, the foam cups and all the rest of the items needed for the morning coffee and muffin customers were ready.

"Matt, you may have heard that I'm opening another restaurant in Darby. Well, it's true. You have been very responsible since you started working for me three years ago, right? I'll need to spend more time in Darby until all the wrinkles are ironed out, and I'd like you to be the manager here on the days that you work. It will mean a little more money, of course. Do you think you're ready for a name tag that says, 'The buck stops here'? I do. By the way, do you know who first said that?"

A good manager accepts responsibility.

ity 41*

Responsible managers honor their word. They can be depended on to keep their commitments.

"Yeah, I do." Matt answered, feeling both excited and anxious at the same time. "It was a sign President Truman had on his desk. He had a small business once, too, as I remember."

"That's right. Next week then, you start as manager whenever you're scheduled. I'll have to hire someone new, but for now I'll see how I can juggle schedules so you won't have to train someone along with your new responsibilities. Are you game to try this?"

"Yes, sir. To be honest, I'm nervous, but thank you for letting me try it."

"Don't be nervous." Mr. Bonito said. "I'm sure you can do it. And I'll only be a cell phone away. But I don't think you'll be calling very often."

The first few weeks everything

People who are responsible:

- keep their promises.
- honor their word and commitments.
- do what is expected of them.
- return what they borrow.
- pay their debts.
- are on time.

The manager of a small store or restaurant must be as reliable as the CEO of a big company.

went pretty smoothly for Matt. Cindy and Kate, the other workers during his shift, were mostly cooperative, but they did some goofing off. Matt sometimes had a tough time figuring out how to make them pay attention to their work without getting them angry with him. Cindy especially liked to try to get away without doing her cleaning and restocking chores before she left at 9:00. And sometimes Matt's buddies

Michael Josephson, founder of the Josephson Institute of Ethics, encourages companies to "hire for character and train for skills." In other words, an employee can learn the necessary work skills—but character is a prerequisite that can't be taught. Josephson says that a shortcoming in any of the core character traits can have a serious impact on business. "If you hire a person that can't be trusted, then people will have to constantly check on that person."

came to the drive-up window and tried to talk him out of some extra fries or a free Coke.

Matt recalled one of Mr. Bonito's sayings whenever he was tempted to give in to one of his pals. "What you allow, you encourage. Don't start something if you think you may want to stop it."

Mr. Bonito had lots of sayings, and most of them were short and to the point. Another one was: "Decision making leads to more decisions, so be sure you make the right one to start out."

Halloween eve and Halloween night were fun times for the little kids, but the teenagers didn't get left out of the special activities in Matt's hometown. The movie theater played old horror movies and

People who demonstrate the character trait of responsibility build trust through their actions. They admit their own mistakes and don't try to cover up, make excuses, or blame someone else. They are organized and careful in their work.

From Working with *Emotional Intelligence* by D. Goleman.

Responsible people stick to their word—even when friends want them to do something else.

the bowling alley next door was set up for games and snacks. Matt hated to miss it, but he was on duty at the BC both nights.

Kevin and Brad pulled up to the drive-in window about 9:00 Halloween night. "When do you and Kate quit work?" Brad yelled.

"The usual time." Matt told him.

"Come on. You don't mean you have to stay tonight? Nobody'll be here. There's curfew for everybody who isn't at *Frankenstein Meets the Mummy*."

"Cindy gets through at 9:30, but we're open until 10:00. Kate and I can't leave until after that."

"We'll come back for Cindy and see if you've changed your mind then." Kevin rolled up the car window, and Brad pulled away.

"Come on, Matt. He's right. You can close early for once. Who's going to know?" Cindy urged.

At 9:30 the boys came back for Cindy. "Sure you won't change your mind?" Kevin said.

"I can't. I'm being paid to be here until 10."

At 9:40, the car pulled up again. All three tried to persuade Matt and Kate to come with them. "Hurry up." Brad was impatient. "If we don't get our curfew passes in five minutes, we're out of luck."

Kate looked pleadingly at Matt. "Make up your own mind, Kate." Matt said. "I can't give you permission to leave—but I can't force you to stay."

It didn't take Kate a minute to peel off her apron and cap and fly out the door to the waiting car. "Last chance," they all called to Matt.

He really wanted to go, but how could he disappoint Mr. Bonito? Matt picked up the broom and dustpan and began sweeping. He had chosen to be a responsible manager.

Only he who keeps his eye fixed on the far horizon will find his right road.

—Dag Hammarskjold

We don't always connect human beings with electronics—but human hands and minds create electronics; the manager of these human beings will often need courage to do what is right for the people he leads.

6

COURAGE

*Sometimes we need to take time to think
before we can act with courage.*

Juan Ramirez was a **human resources** department manager for the Comco Electronics assembly plant. He was invited to many executive board meetings even though his was a nonvoting position. This Monday morning there was tension in the faces and body language of the board members even before the meeting started.

Teresa Bonti, quality control manager, looked at Juan, and whispered, "What's going on?" Juan just shrugged. Everyone seated at the conference table kept their eyes down and fidgeted with papers and pens, then jumped nervously when Mark Lovell, vice president and plant manager, came in and slammed his clipboard on the conference table. He got right to the point of the meeting.

"The company is moving some assembly production to Korea and closing one line. We have to lay off 35 people in manufacturing. It doesn't look like it will affect supervisory or management positions at this time, so you're all safe for now. The cuts will take place this month, possibly starting as soon as Friday."

"But why?" Teresa asked. "We put out good assemblies. We have lots of orders. Our customers trust our quality."

"Isn't this awfully sudden?" Juan added. "Which line is going to be shut down?"

Maintaining employee morale is an important part of a manager's job.

"This is all I can tell you right now. The move is being made for economic reasons. You know how many other plants around here have laid off and relocated for the sake of their bottom line. I want you all to understand, this is strictly confidential—for obvious reasons. The effect on employee **morale** will only make the situation worse, so we don't want any internal gossip until the layoff slips are handed out, and we need to avoid the possibilities of sabotage and pilfering. According to company policy, those who are terminated will be escorted to their lockers and then directly to the parking lot, as usual. There are to be absolutely no leaks from this meeting. Any outside discussion of what was said here today will be cause for disciplinary action regardless of your position. Understood?"

Recognizing a Moral Issue

Is there conflict that could be damaging to people?
Does the issue go deeper than selfish concerns?
Could the dignity and rights of others be harmed?

It was a short meeting. As they left the conference room, Teresa Bonti tugged at Juan's sleeve.

"Do you think this is real?" she asked. "Or another of the so-called confidences that gets leaked to the press to scare the production crew out of asking for more benefits?"

"I can't say for sure, but my personnel department has been in a hiring freeze for almost two months."

"I didn't know that." Teresa continued. "What else do you know?"

"No more than you do, and if I did, I couldn't say." Juan turned to go into his office. "This could be rough. Not many jobs out there right now."

He absently sifted through the memos on his desk, troubled by thoughts of the layoffs. Some of those who would soon be unemployed had passed through the personnel office while he was manager. He might have added their new babies to their health insurance plans, helped with paperwork when they married or became citizens, or just listened as they complained about a problem with a coworker.

Managers may be responsible for piles of paperwork—but that paperwork often represents the lives of many individuals.

Juan's phone rang, interrupting his thoughts. The woman on the other end of the line was the loan manager of a finance company and needed some routine information. She was about to give final approval for a Comco employee to mortgage his home. Juan confirmed that the man indeed worked for Comco, that he was a full-time employee, and also verified his hourly and weekly income. He knew what the woman's final question would be and dreaded it.

"What is the probability of Dick Sandler's continued employment?" the woman asked.

Juan raked his fingers through his hair. His heart was beating faster. He wished he had more time to think before answering.

What would you say in his position?

If Juan tells the loan officer that the worker's probability of continued employment is average, would he be lying? If he answers that way, within days Dick Sandler will sign a contract that would put him at risk of losing his home if he is one of those to be laid off and can't find another job. If Juan tries to delay answering the question, the finance

A good manager has the courage to look beyond the numbers to the people those numbers will affect.

Courageous managers dare to use their power to lend a hand to others.

People with courage. . .

- present themselves with self-assurance.
- are decisive; in other words, they are able to make good decisions despite uncertainties and pressures.
- can voice views that are unpopular and go out on a limb for what is right.
- are loyal to friends and associates, even if they are on the less popular side of an issue.
- are not intimidated by people with wealth or power—and neither do they use their own power for unfair advantage.
- lead by example.
- challenge the status quo if they see the need for change.

An elderly man had a stroke because he hadn't been taking his blood pressure medicine. Now he was in the intensive care unit (ICU), and the next few days would tell whether he would live or die. The nurse looked at his chart and noticed that among the many medicines prescribed for him, there wasn't one to control his blood pressure. Concerned, she brought it to the attention of the neurologist looking at the results of the man's brain scan. "We only treat the brain here," he snapped. "I'm not in charge of the rest of his body."

The nurse then went to the head nurse in charge of the ICU and told her what had happened and why she questioned the doctor. The head nurse replied that if the doctor wasn't concerned, that should be the end of it. It was best not to challenge the doctor. The first nurse then went to the office of the chief of medicine at the hospital, apologized for interrupting his busy schedule, and brought the situation to his attention. He went to the ICU, reviewed the patient's chart, and ordered the proper blood pressure medication. Lucky for the patient, the hospital's manager had enough courage to challenge the **status quo.**

company may sense something is wrong and start a rumor that will damage the company and the community.

If the loan officer is made aware of the coming job cuts and Mr. Sandler is not laid off, it could ruin the chance he will get the needed mortgage anyway. Disclosing information to the bank will violate the confidentiality of the board meeting and jeopardize Juan's own position. He was warned that anyone leaking information about the layoffs would be disciplined. Could he be demoted or even fired from his job? Does he have the courage he needs to face the consequences of his actions—whatever decision he makes?

There are many situations in which those in management positions need the courage to balance the rights or needs of one group against those of another. You may have hours or days to make a decision about your actions or you may need to answer in just minutes, as Juan did. That's one reason why practicing good character every day is important. With practice you form habits; you learn how to weigh the principles of good character to make a decision.

Sometimes it helps to use a checklist to work out a moral dilemma:

- Did you **clarify**? Did you decide exactly what it is that needs to be decided and list the full range of alternatives? For example, did you eliminate the impractical and illegal options?
- Did you **evaluate**? If any of the options require the sacrifice of an ethical principle, be careful to reevaluate. Did you distinguish solid facts from beliefs, desires, and opinions that might be false or self-interested? Did you consider the burdens, benefits, and risks?
- Did you **decide**? Did you put your options in priority order and consider who will be helped the most and harmed the least? Did you use these three "ethics guides"?

When an ethical dilemma presents itself, you may have only a few minutes to reach a decision.

Golden Rule: Are you treating others as you would want to be treated?

Publicity: Would you be comfortable if your reasoning and decision were on the front page of the newspaper?

Friend or Relative on Your Shoulder: Would you be comfortable explaining your action to your mother, best friend, little sister, or religious leader?

- Did you **implement**? Once you decide, you must act.
- Will you **monitor and modify**? Once you put a plan into action, you must be willing and prepared to revise it or take a different course of action if new information is presented.

How do you think Juan could apply this checklist to his situation?

Lose not courage, lose not faith, go forward.

—Marcus Garvey

Using a "carrot" to motivate workers is often more effective than the "stick"—but it takes self-discipline and diligence to learn more positive management techniques.

7

SELF-DISCIPLINE AND DILIGENCE

*What is the difference between working
hard—and diligent self-discipline?*

A t well past 5:00, Michelle Wong sat at her desk at the radio station balancing her personal checkbook. She had been saving regularly, and soon would be taking a vacation. The only problem was the work that kept piling up on her desk. But she still loved being the advertising manager for WAOK. The radio station was gaining in the ratings and more businesses were willing to spend money on commercials.

Michelle supervised two sales representatives, but some of the original clients she had called on when she was a salesperson preferred that she continue to handle their accounts. She worked long hours, driving to her clients' businesses, taking them to lunch, and asking about their families. Her evenings were spent at home researching and designing creative advertising that would get good results. Her boss probably never guessed how much work she took home at night in order to meet deadlines.

As overworked as she felt, she was often impatient when her salespeople needed her to help rewrite some advertising copy. Sometimes she was short-tempered when they were discouraged about losing a sale. She just didn't have enough time in her day to spend doling out sympathy. Somehow, though, her work always got done on time— sometimes, just in time. Her last-minute miracles kept the production staff and disc jockeys on edge, especially when background music or a company's ad jingles were ordered late. Express mail and special courier delivery seemed to be the rule since Michelle became manager.

Now, she looked with dismay at her untidy desk. She really needed this vacation with her sister, but how could she get her workload under control so she dared to leave for a week?

George McNeil, the station owner, tapped on her open office door. "Can I come in for a minute? You know, I think you make things harder than they are. You look overwhelmed at times. Can't you delegate some of this to Barry and Maggie?"

Michelle felt apprehensive. "Have you had any complaints?" she questioned. "I thought my work was satisfactory. Oh, you mean this mess?" She made an effort to straighten some of the piles of papers. "I was rewriting some of the copy for All-Star Tractor. Barry's scripts always run a few seconds too long. It's easier for me to do it once, than to have him redo it four or five times."

Dealing with paperwork is a task that requires self-discipline and diligence.

Instead of trying to do everything herself, a good manager knows when to pass a responsibility on to someone else.

"But he's responsible for getting it done, Michelle. It's what he gets paid for. And if he has trouble, he should go to Andrea. Copywriting is her job.

"I don't mind," Michelle replied. "All-Star used to be my client and I know what works for them. Is that a problem?"

"Well, yes and no. I certainly appreciate your dedication to your work and to WAOK, but you must feel the stress of trying to keep up with everything—and sometimes that stress trickles down to your staff." Mr. McNeil continued. "Ready Rate Insurance is considering buying some air time from us and I don't know if you can add it to your workload. I know you pride yourself on

---

People with self-discipline. . .

- do what they say they will do.
- do not give in to temptation or distraction.
- take action to fix their mistakes.
- are willing to take on challenges.
- can delay short-term satisfaction in pursuit of long-term goals.

Adapted from the Josephson Institute of Ethics.

A diligent manager may sometimes need to participate in a class or workshop to hone her skills.

Self-discipline sometimes means giving up control, standing back, and letting others try. Becoming a mentor, which means leading others through the steps of learning, can be very rewarding.

A manager must be willing to lead but is not responsible for coming up with all the answers.
—Michael Josephson

being self-taught and your theater background helps you come up with creative advertising spots. Can I make a suggestion about the management part of your job?"

"Yes, of course." Michelle felt a warm flush of pleasure at the recognition of her talents, but also a twinge of resentment at the criticism of her efforts.

Mr. McNeil put a brochure on her desk. "I thought you might find this of interest. The county community college is hosting a series of seminars on management techniques." Mr. McNeil said good night and left the room.

The lecturers were famous people in the business world across the country. She looked at the titles of the courses:

Is the Top of Your Desk a Fire Hazard?
Are You a Supervisor or a Baby-Sitter?
How to Love Your Job Without Marrying It.
How to be a Mentor to Your Employees.

The workshops certainly sounded more interesting than the usual business seminars. She looked at the seminar date. It was the same week as the holiday she had planned.

Her mind raced as she stuffed broadcast schedules in a folder to take home. She cringed at the idea of postponing her vacation. But she found herself wondering if in the long run, the seminars might make her feel less overworked than any holiday could ever accomplish.

Self-discipline sometimes means admitting you need to learn more; diligence means you make time to learn.

Dave Thomas, founder of Wendy's restaurants says:

Never stop learning. Graduation doesn't mean the end of learning, it's just the beginning. The "real world" has so much to teach us—only if we are ready and willing to take notes.

Do what makes you happy. Whether it's choosing a career or deciding what charity to get involved with, the choice should come from your heart. Ultimately, you are the one who has to get up every morning and enjoy what you are doing, so make sure it matters to you.

Break out of your routine. Doing things the way you always have done them can only get you where you've already been. Don't be afraid to shake things up and try something new.

Live life to the fullest. Many times we focus on accomplishing our goals and don't take time to celebrate our achievements. Don't miss an opportunity to spend times with your family and friends—they're an important part of your life.

Believe in yourself. You have come this far, so have the courage to continue to learn and grow. If you believe in yourself, you can achieve all your goals.

From News USA, Inc., *Dave Thomas Addresses Graduates.*

What would you decide to do if you were Michelle?

Is it possible to work too hard? What do you think? Is Michelle demonstrating professional self-discipline and diligence when she works such long hours? Or are these character qualities she has yet to learn? How could she practice these traits?

Self-discipline and diligence are the quiet virtues. . . .

Harry had nearly perfect scores on his SATs. He knew he was smart, won a scholarship, and chose a top university. He often skipped class, turned papers in late, dropped out of college, and finally graduated after ten years. He struggled in a one-man computer consulting business. He failed to return clients' phone calls and frequently did not keep appointments. He was smart, but he lacked self-discipline.

Jon, his high school classmate was an average student in most subjects but had a keen interest in computers. Jon worked very hard at understanding programming, even giving up football so he could go to computer camp in the summer. He worked in his uncle's hardware store to earn money for college. When he graduated, he trained with the state police and programmed a computer system to more quickly track criminals around the country.

It takes self-discipline to juggle all our interests, responsibilities, and talents.

The Marshmallow Test

What it lies in our power to do, it lies our power not to do.
  —Aristotle

Four-year-olds were brought into a room one at a time. A marshmallow was put on a plate in front of them. They were told they could eat it if they wanted to, but if they waited until the adult left the room for a few minutes and then came back, they could have two marshmallows.

Fourteen years later, as these same children graduated from high school, researchers found that those who grabbed the first marshmallow lost their tempers more easily and were more likely to give in to temptations and lose sight of their goals.

Those who, as four-year-olds, waited and were rewarded for their self-discipline with two marshmallows were not only more diligent and better able to say no to temptations when they were in their teens, they scored over 200 points higher on the college entrance exam.

Adapted from *Working with Emotional Intelligence*, D. Goleman.

Diligence is the mother of good luck.

—Benjamin Franklin

Self-discipline is when your conscience tells you to do something and you don't talk back.

—W. K. Hope

No store or business stands alone; they are knit together into an intertwined community.

8

CITIZENSHIP

*I pledge: My head to clearer thinking,
my heart to greater loyalty, my hands
to larger service, my health to better
living, for my club, my community,
my country, and my world.*
—4-H Club Pledge

Sandy Barker's list of businesses to visit was a long one. Luckily, she knew most of the people in her small hometown and wasn't shy about asking for donations for the Strawberry Festival. The two-day event would be held for the fourth year and everyone looked forward to the ice cream, children's games, baking contest, raffles, and the used-book sale. Every year the celebration got bigger and raised more money for the library; but growing also meant it took more money to buy supplies, rent tents, have T-shirts printed, and pay for all the other expenses that had to be covered before the festival even started. More and more people were needed to do face painting, blow up balloons, cook hamburgers, and cart boxes of heavy books to the village green once the weekend activities got underway. And, as so often happens in any town, the same people pitched in to help every time, for every community occasion.

Sandy walked confidently into Vernon Bank and Trust bank to keep her appointment with Mark Hendren, the vice president and manager of

A manager needs to make the difficult decision about how funds can be best used to benefit the most people.

the main branch. He had written generous checks to the festival committee in the past as seed money for expenses. Mr. Hendren's smile was genuine as he listened to Sandy list the things they needed to buy for the new children's games they would be setting up this year. They needed lumber and paint for the miniature golf course and fish pond, prizes for pee-wee basketball, and so much more. Families enjoyed the festival and the library raised a significant part of the money needed for new books and computers.

How would you answer these questions today?

• *Is my community better because I was in it?*
• *Am I better because I was in my community?*

(What is my community? My family, apartment building, neighborhood, club, church, school.)

"This has been quite a demanding year as far as donations are concerned." Mr. Hendron leaned back in his chair, tapping a silver pen on his mouse pad. "We, meaning the bank, have always tried to support the local nonprofit organizations as much as possible. Are you finding it more difficult to get support, what with the Red Cross disaster fund and hospital building program? It seems to me that hardly a day goes by without a request for a donation for a walkathon or spaghetti dinner or jamboree for some cause or another."

Sandy sat very still, trying not to look alarmed. What was he trying to tell her? "Yes, but the library and preschool reading programs seem to be a priority to many people. And the festival brings people from outside the county, so the

People who are good citizens. . .

- vote.
- voice their opinions.
- cooperate with the majority opinion (as long as it doesn't contradict their conscience).
- obey all laws, even if they disagree with them.
- work to change laws that they see as unfair.
- volunteer.
- do good deeds with no expectation of being paid back.
- respect the environment.
- are good neighbors.

When a bank manager approves a loan, he is helping his community flourish.

Is there a **civic** question or problem about which you have strong feelings? Have you written a letter to a newspaper about it? Do you know how to contact or write to your elected officials?

money we raise isn't all from the local people who are asked to give again and again whenever someone has a misfortune, like a house fire or catastrophic illness."

He pulled the bank checkbook ceremoniously out from the desk drawer and began to write. Sandy relaxed a little and was already checking her list for her next stop when Mr. Hendren stopped writing and closed the book without tearing out the check.

"No," he said. "I can't do this before I talk to some people. Can you come back tomorrow? No, better make it Thursday."

"Of course." Sandy tried not to look disappointed. She thought Mr. Hendren had the authority to write the check, but maybe bank policy had changed. Maybe he was going to write a larger check than usual

Managers work with others to create something good for the entire community.

Who are really important people?
The rich are often not admired.
The famous may soon be forgotten.
Celebrities, though known to millions, may be lonely.

Can you name:
The five richest people in the world?
The last four Super Bowl MVPs?
The last three pairs of teams in the Stanley Cup finals?
The best-selling recording star of three years ago?

Now . . . can you name:
The two teachers who made you want to do your best in
    their class?
Three friends who stood by you during difficult times?
Four people who appreciate you or make you feel special?
Four people whose stories would make you call them
    heroes?

and needed to consult his superiors. Maybe the bank budget for donations was smaller and he couldn't write a check at all.

"I'll see you Thursday at about this same time. Is that all right?"
Sandy tried to sound upbeat.

He nodded and walked her to the door, looking thoughtful.

The next few days, Sandy found herself getting discouraged. Some
donations were smaller than in previous years. The people she talked to
were supportive, but it had been a hard year for the small community.

Sandy knocked timidly at Mr. Hendren's office door Thursday
afternoon.

"Come in. Have a seat." He gestured at a chair and sat back down
behind his desk. "I spoke to a few board members and have a proposi-
tion for you."

Sandy tensed. The library's checking account was at the rival bank

In addition to individual citizenship, there is also corporate citizenship. Workers who have a stake in a company, whether they are owners, managers, or stockholders, can contribute to the ethical and moral mission of the company. They are often inspired by the goals of the company's leaders who have a high level of commitment to their job. One worker said, "I get called by other companies all they time with offers to hire me away from IBM. They say 'We can make you very rich.' But they don't get it. I am going to change the world with this [work]. I'm making a difference."

Money may not be as important as the chance to make a difference in the world.

> ### Lions International's Goals
>
> - To create and foster a spirit of understanding among the peoples of the world.
> - To promote the principle of good government and good citizenship.
> - To take an active interest in the civic, cultural, social, and moral welfare of the community.
> - To unite the clubs in the bonds of friendship, good fellowship, and mutual understanding.
> - To provide a forum for the open discussion of all matters of public interest; provided, however, that partisan politics and sectarian religion shall not be debated by club members.
> - To encourage service-minded people to serve their community without personal financial reward, and to encourage efficiency and promote high ethical standards in commerce, industry, professions, public works, and private endeavors.

downtown. She hoped Mr. Hendren wasn't going to withhold a large donation unless they changed their account.

"I'll be writing a smaller check this year," he continued.

Sandy's smile was frozen on her face. "I understand. We appreciate anything you can do."

"Well," Mr. Hendren went on. "I don't think you understand, but I'll explain what I have in mind. Writing a check is easy compared to the job you and your volunteer committee have to do to pull off this festival. We decided, if you agree, that we will pay our employees for four hours if they want to take that time and work at the festival instead of at the bank. This will encourage our employees to be good citizens in our community. I think it's a win-win situation all the way around. What do you think?"

"I think that's great! Thank you." Sandy stood up, elated.

"There's just one string attached." Mr. Hendren grinned. "I want to work in the ice cream booth on my shift."

How do you think Mr. Hendren's behavior might influence employee behavior?

Do you think his actions will influence other business managers in the county?

How would you respond if your school or club announced they would no longer collect money, hold walk-a-thons, or sell things to earn donations for charities, but you had to perform community service instead? What service would you choose?

We cannot live only for ourselves. A thousand fibers connect us with our fellow [human beings].

—Herman Melville

The business world is full of management opportunities.

9

CAREER OPPORTUNITIES

*Good managers show others the
right road to follow.*

Dave Thomas knew since he was a teenager that he wanted to own his own restaurant. He didn't expect to be the owner and manager of a chain of nearly 4,000 restaurants, but that's where his talent and character took him.

Molly worked at the front desk of a large hotel on weekends to pay for her college tuition. She studied English, psychology, and art history with no clear idea of what she wanted to do with her adult life. She observed the organization that went into planning various functions in the hotel's conference center. The people who used the facilities for corporate business meetings were stimulating and energized but sometimes demanding. The wedding receptions were beautiful and fun but often nerve-racking. She told her supervisor that she was willing to help with these affairs even though it was beyond her job description to do so. Soon the sense of pride in dealing with the inevitable last-minute requests and helping each event go smoothly convinced her that her future lay in hotel management. She added accounting and marketing to her liberal arts studies and got additional experience in a summer position at a resort.

When Lee Iococca was a small boy, he earned money by waiting outside the neighborhood grocery store with his red wagon and then hauling bags of food to the housewives' homes for the tips they gave him. His *entrepreneurial* spirit showed early, but his real fascination was with the design of cars and trucks. After earning a degree in industrial engineering, he worked for Ford Motor Company, was responsible for the design of the original Mustang, and eventually became president of Ford. A disagreement with Henry Ford II resulted in Iocacca being fired, but within weeks he was offered the challenge of rescuing Chrysler Corporation from near bankruptcy. Many of Iococca's associates from Ford, including his secretary, quit their jobs to follow him, even though they risked their retirement pensions. His management style was decisive, honest, and plainspoken. The people who worked for him trusted him, and they were as loyal to him as he was to them.

Nordstrom's is a large department, store well known on the west coast for its good quality clothing brands and outstanding service. Patrick McCarthy was the store's star salesperson in menswear. Literally hundreds of customers asked for him when they had special requests. He went out of his way to remember his clients' color prefer-

If a manager of a car dealership makes an effort to get to know his customers, his business will be more successful.

Check out the Internet for more information on management careers.

The Internet provides a fun and interesting way to pretend you are looking for a management career. Go to a search engine such as Google, Yahoo, or Excite and enter a **company name** or a **profession** or **job**, then add **management** or **manager** and **employment**.

Your entry could look like this: **Hershey+manager+employment** and you will see if the chocolate company is looking for any managers. They will tell you what education and experience they would like you to have, and also whether the job is located in the town in Pennsylvania that smells like chocolate or in Dallas, Texas.

Try entering your country's government instead of a company and you find opportunities, including those in foreign countries.

Small shops all have managers. If you're interested in a career in management, job opportunities are everywhere!

ences and other details. He was promoted to department manager and performed satisfactorily from Nordstrom's point of view. But one year later, Mr. McCarthy asked to be relieved of his duties and to be allowed to go back to sales.

Managers come in many forms—but why is this last anecdote included? Doesn't it demonstrate the failure of someone in a management position?

Many people think of management as a natural step up in the working world. They assume that the worker at the front counter at a fast food restaurant will eventually be offered a position as shift manager or a bank teller who demonstrates accuracy, punctuality, and responsibility may be promoted to accounts manager. It is true that job experience can put you in line to be a supervisor or manager. Management, however, can be a separate career requiring certain talents, aptitudes, and personality traits. Very few teachers aspire to be a school principal; not every policeman wishes to be chief of police. This does not mean that

A Description of a Highly Ethical Organization

- Members are obsessed with fairness. The ground rules state that the other person's interests count as much as their own.
- Individuals are responsible to themselves.
- Integrity rules the system of rewards.
- Policies and practices agree with the vision. There are no mixed messages.
- Character pillars are not just window-dressing to improve public image; they are put into practice regularly.

The manager of the grocery store meat department has plenty of opportunities to demonstrate his character.

According to a 2002 article in the *Baltimore Sun,* Professor Stephen Loeb of the University of Maryland's School of Business takes his classes on a field trip to prisons where the people serving their sentences have committed crimes while in business. Some of these criminals were in high places in management. As a student or beginner in the business world, it's easy to think that cutting corners is part of the way things are done. The prisoners tell the students how tempting it is, once you've crossed the line from ethical to unethical behavior, to cross again and again . . . until you find yourself permanently on the wrong side.

Professor Loeb says: "Business ethics as a course of study tends to take a backseat because it doesn't seem to make you money. But ultimately the people who are ethical are the ones who prosper in part because they stay out of trouble. Not only do they stay out of trouble with the law, they can spend their energy going forward because they don't have to keep looking back to see if they've been caught. Character does count."

these people aren't bright enough or that they do not work hard. They simply prefer the job they are doing.

How many different jobs and careers are there in the field of management?

The list is almost unlimited. Think of anyone who owns a business or provides a service and employs or supervises even one other person besides herself, and you have found a manager. How many can you add to this list?

- Nursing home administrator
- Insurance agent
- District attorney
- Car dealer

- Funeral director
- Newspaper editor
- Chemical company executive
- Sports arena manager
- Thoroughbred farm manager
- Construction foreman
- Director of the American Red Cross
- Prime minister of Canada or president of the United States
- Armed forces officer
- Advertising executive
- TV producer
- 911 coordinator
- Human resources specialist
- Cruise ship captain
- Fire chief

When you walk down any street, every store or business you pass has a manager.

Job opportunities for skilled professional managers continue to grow as the world's business and government become more complex and intertwined. Think of the exciting challenges awaiting managers who, in order to do their jobs, must travel to foreign countries and learn respect for other cultures and ideas.

The stereotype of men as managers and women as their employees or secretaries no longer holds true. Look around you and you will find women as managers in many small businesses and in government offices. Not as visible to most people are the women who now hold responsible, high-ranking positions in large companies. Women have been the CEOs (chief executive officers) of such well-known companies as Mattel and Hewlett Packard.

Whatever your gender, as a manager you can make a difference in the world. With your leadership and encouragement, you can show others the road to follow—the road that leads to a strong sense of right and wrong, moral choices, and a life that's based on the habits of good character.

Almost anyone can stand adversity. To test a person's strength of character, give him [or her] power.

—Abraham Lincoln

FURTHER READING

Blanchard, Kenneth and Spencer Johnson. *The One Minute Manager.* New York: Morrow, 1982.

Covey, Stephen R. *The Seven Habits of Highly Effective People: Restoring the Character Ethic.* New York: Simon and Schuster, 1989.

Goleman, Daniel. *Working With Emotional Intelligence.* New York: Bantam Books, 1998.

Josephson, Michael S. and Wes Hanson, editors. *The Power of Character.* San Francisco: Jossey-Bass, 1998.

Kidder, Rushworth M. *How Good People Make Tough Choices.* New York: Simon & Schuster, 1995.

Peters, Thomas J. *In Search of Excellence.* New York: Harper & Row, 1982.

Thomas, R. David. *Dave Says. . . . Well Done.* New York: Harper Collins, 1994.

Thomas, R. David. *Dave's Way.* New York: Berkeley Publishing Group, 1992.

For More Information

American Management Association
135 West 50th Street
New York, New York 10020

Central Michigan University College of Business Administration
mkt.cba.cmich.edu/careers

The Centre for Applied Ethics
University of British Columbia
227-6356 Agricultural Road
Vancouver, B.C. Canada, V6T 1Z2
www.ethics.ubc.ca

Complete Guide to Ethics Management: An Ethics Toolkit for Managers by
Carter McNamara, MBA, Ph.D.
www.mapnp.org/library/ethics

Occupational Outlook Handbook, The Bureau of Labor Statistics
www.bis.gov/oco

GLOSSARY

Acumen Shrewdness; keen perception.

Burned out Emotionally exhausted.

Civic Having to do with citizenship or your responsibilities to your community.

Down syndrome A condition caused by a defect in the human chromosome that causes mental retardation.

Entrepreneurial Having to do with business.

Ethical dilemma A situation that requires a person to make a choice about what is right and wrong.

Ethics The principles of what is right and wrong that govern the behavior of both individuals and groups.

Global economy The worldwide production, consumption, and distribution of goods and money.

Great Depression The period of American history from 1929 to 1939, when there was low general economic activity and high rates of unemployment.

Human resources Personnel.

Morale The mental and emotional condition (as of enthusiasm, confidence, or loyalty) of a group of workers for their task.

Remuneration Payment.

Stakeholders People who have something to win or lose in a given situation.

Status quo The way things are; the existing state of affairs.

Turnover Change in employees.

Vocational Having to do with employment or occupation.

INDEX

BIOGRAPHIES

Ann Vitale owns and manages a new car dealership with her husband John. Before joining him in the business, she used her university education as a microbiologist and worked in a medical center. She lives in the country in northeast Pennsylvania with a Newfoundland dog and a calico cat. Ann is a 4-H leader and for 25 years has taught dog care and training to young people and their pets.

Cheryl Gholar is a Community and Economic Development Educator with the University of Illinois Extension. She has a Ph.D. in Educational Leadership and Policy Studies from Loyola University, and she has more than 20 years of experience with the Chicago Public Schools as a teacher, counselor, guidance coordinator, and administrator. Recognized for her expertise in the field of character education, Dr. Gholar assisted in developing the K–12 Character Education Curriculum for the Chicago Public Schools, and she is a five-year participant in the White House Conference on Character Building for a Democratic and Civil Society. The recipient of numerous awards, she is also the author of *Beyond Rhetoric and Rainbows: A Journey to the Place Where Learning Lives.*

Ernestine G. Riggs is an Assistant Professor at Loyola University Chicago and a Senior Program Consultant for the North Central Regional Educational Laboratory. She has a Ph.D. in Educational Leadership and Policy Studies from Loyola University, and she has been involved in the field of education for more than 35 years. An advocate of teaching the whole child, she is a frequent presenter at district and national conferences; she also serves as a consultant for several state boards of education. Dr. Riggs has received many citations, including an award from the United States Department of Defense Overseas Schools for Outstanding Elementary Teacher of America.